Reptiles
and amphibians

P9-DHB-918

UNIV OF MOUNT U
CURRICULUM CENTE

what is a reptile?

Turtles and tortoises

Reptiles have existed since before the dinosaurs lived, and some are among the most poisonous and dangerous animals on Earth. There are many different reptiles but they all have scaly skin, cold blood and lay eggs.

Crocodilians

Snakes

Lizards

what is an amphibian?

Most amphibians live in both water and on land. Nearly all of them begin life in water, swimming and breathing like fish. The best known amphibians are frogs and toads, and salamanders and newts.

Salamanders and newts

Frogs and toads

The Komodo Dragon is the world's largest lizard. The really big ones can be 10 feet (3 m) long and weigh as much as 155 lb (70 kg). They hunt big animals such as deer and have poisonous saliva to help kill their prey.

Average length: 7 ft (2.1 m)

Danger rating

Very long forked tongue flicks out when it is looking for food

Sharp claws used for digging up food and burrowing into the ground

Komodo dragon

Green iguana

Spiky scales along its back

Average length: 4.5 ft (1.3 m)

Danger rating

The green iguana is a large lizard that lives in the jungles of Central and South America. They spend most of their time high up in the trees, where their color keeps them hidden among the leaves.

Only the male has this flap of skin, called a dewlap

Chameleon

Skin becomes darker when they are cold and need to warm up

These unusual reptiles have extremely long tongues, which they use to catch insects. They can also change the color of their skin according to changes in light, temperature and the mood they are in!

Eyes can be moved in any direction

Tongue has an extremely sticky tip

Average length: 16 in (40 cm)
Danger rating

Water dragon

Row of small spikes along its back

Average length: 3 ft (91 cm)

Danger rating

☠ ☠ ☠ ☠ ☠

Water dragons are large lizards that live in Southeast Asia and Australia. They love to bask in the sun close to water, and being excellent swimmers, they will run into the water to escape from predators.

Pink chin and neck

Toe pads are so sticky that the gecko can even hang upside down

Geckos are small lizards with the amazing ability to climb walls using sticky pads on their toes. They are also able to make very loud noises, which they use to scare predators and attract mates.

Gecko

Average length: 8 in (20 cm)

Danger rating

Frilled lizard

The middle of the frill is bright orange

This spectacular looking lizard from **Australia** has a large scaly frill around its neck. It opens up the **frill** and hisses loudly to **frighten** off predators, then quickly runs up a **tree** to hide.

Average length: 26 in (66 cm)

Danger rating

Thorny devil

Spikes to defend and disguise itself

The **thorny** devil gets its name from the rows of sharp spikes that completely cover its body. The spiked armor helps this slow-moving lizard defend itself against predators.

Sharp toothless beak

Average length: 7 in (18 cm)

Danger rating

Plumed basilisk

Average length: 27 in (66 cm)

Danger rating

Wide feet help to spread its weight

Long tail adds support when running on water

The plumed basilisk is a bright green lizard that lives in the jungles of Mexico and other parts of Central America. It can run across the surface of water on its back legs, earning it the nickname 'Jesus lizard.'

Blue-tongued skink

Average length: 19 in (48 cm)

Danger rating

Toothless but powerful mouth

Short legs

This large Australian lizard moves very slowly and spends most of its time basking in the sun. When it is threatened, it hisses loudly and sticks out its bright blue tongue.

Emerald tree boa

Vertical pupils help it to detect its prey

The **emerald** tree boa lives in the trees in South American **jungles,** where its beautiful green **color** helps it hide among the leaves. It **coils** itself around a branch, ready to **strike** at small mammals and birds.

White markings along its back

Average length: 6 ft (1.8 m)

Danger rating

Boa constrictor

Average length: 7 ft (2.1 m)

Danger rating

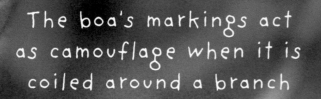

The boa's markings act as camouflage when it is coiled around a branch

Dark stripe behind each eye

The boa constrictor is a very large snake found in many parts of South America, from jungles and swamps to dry grasslands and even towns! They kill their prey by wrapping themselves around it and squeezing until it suffocates. Some of the biggest boas can be as long as a car!

Flat head and large eyes

This **African** snake moves very quickly through **grassland** and up trees, where its greenish **coloring** makes it very hard to see. It is not poisonous, but will strike out and **bite** fiercely if threatened.

Average length: 3.2 ft (1 m)
Danger rating

Spotted bush snake

Dark spots along skin

The rattlesnake is a very poisonous snake. In the USA, the western diamondback 'rattler' is responsible for most snake bites among people. It uses the horny rattle at the end of its tail to warn off predators.

Average length: 6.5 ft (2 m)

Danger rating

Fangs in its mouth inject venom into its prey

Buzzing rattle made from old skin

Rattlesnake

cobra

Average length: 5 ft (1.5 m)

Danger rating

The cobra's hood is made from muscle and skin

A cobra's **hood** makes it one of the most familiar snakes, and these are the types often used by snake **charmers.** All of them are very **poisonous** and some of them can even spit **venom** from their **fangs!**

Galapagos tortoise

This very large tortoise lives only on the Galapagos Islands off the coast of South America. It can be up to 4 ft (1.2 m) long and live to well over 100 years old.

The tortoise's huge outer shell is called a carapace

Neck can stretch up to reach bushes to eat

Average length: 3 ft (1 m)
Danger rating

Sea turtle

These reptiles spend most of their time in the sea, where they are known to swim great distances across the oceans. They have no teeth, but use their sharp beaks to chew on plants, fish and even shellfish.

Average length: 3 ft (1 m)
Danger rating

Four powerful flippers

Streamlined shell helps it to swim quickly

Crocodile

Crocodiles are large **meat-eating** reptiles that live mostly in **freshwater** rivers and lakes in Africa, Asia and Australia. They have very **powerful** jaws filled with **sharp** teeth, which they use to hunt fish, and larger animals at the water's edge.

Eyes on top of its head allow it to see while hiding in the water

Crocodiles have a very hard bite but they cannot chew

Average length: 16 ft (5 m)
Danger rating

Alligator

Average length: 12 ft (3.6 m)

Danger rating

Tough bony plates along its back

Webbed feet are good for swimming

The difference between an alligator and a crocodile is that an alligator has a shorter snout and its lower teeth are hidden when its mouth is closed. Alligators live in the lakes and swamps of the southern USA and parts of Central and South America.

Red-eyed tree frog

Average length: 2 in (5 cm)

Danger rating

Large, bright red eyes

Sticky toe pads for climbing trees

This **brightly-colored** frog lives in the trees in the jungles of Central America. If it is **disturbed** while asleep, its eyelids pop open and its bright red eyes **frighten** off any would-be predator.

The marine toad, or cane toad, is the biggest toad in the world. It comes from Central and South America but also lives in parts of Australia. It produces large amounts of very powerful poison from behind its shoulders.

Average length: 5.5 in (14 cm)

Danger rating

Large, bony ridges over each eye

Marine toad

White's tree frog

White's **tree** frog comes from Australia but has been **introduced** to many other parts of the world. These funny-looking **amphibians** are one of the most popular types of **pet** frogs.

Big head and rounded body

Large, sticky toe pads

Shiny, waxy skin

Average length: 3 in (7.5 cm)

Danger rating

Poison-dart frog

Very powerful poison comes through its skin

These frogs can be blue, green, red or yellow

Average length: 2 in (5 cm)
Danger rating

The incredible colors of this South American jungle frog warn its predators how poisonous it is. Its name comes from the local tribes who use the poison on darts, which they use for hunting.

These large, noisy frogs are famous for eating huge amounts of insects, small mammals and even other frogs! The male bullfrog has an inflatable sac under its throat that it uses to make very loud mating calls.

Large eardrums

Average length: 5 in (13 cm)
Danger rating

Inflatable sac

Bullfrog

The strikingly-colored fire salamander is an amphibian that spends its time entirely out of water, living in forests, hills and woodland. It produces a mild poison which makes it taste nasty to anything that tries to eat it.

Poison is produced in glands behind its ears

Average length: 9 in (23 cm)
Danger rating

Fire salamander

Glossary

Camouflage Where an animal's skin is a similar color to its surroundings, helping it to hide.

Claw A sharp curved nail on an animal's toe used for tearing, digging and scratching.

Cold-blooded Animals whose blood temperature changes with the temperature of their surroundings are 'cold-blooded'.

Fang The long, sharp and hollow tooth of a poisonous snake used to inject venom into prey.

Flipper A broad flat limb used for swimming.

Gland An part of an animal that produces a substance, for example, venom.